SWEDEN

GROLIER
EDUCATIONAL

Published 1999 by Grolier Educational
Sherman Turnpike, Danbury, Connecticut.
Copyright © 1999 Times Editions Pte Ltd. Singapore.

Set ISBN: 0-7172-9324-6
Volume ISBN: 0-7172-9334-3

CIP information available from the Library of Congress or the publisher

Brown Partworks Ltd.

Series Editor: Tessa Paul
Series Designer: Joyce Mason
Crafts devised and created by Susan Moxley
Music arrangements by Harry Boteler
Photographs by Bruce Mackie
Subeditor: Annette Cheyne
Production: Alex Mackenzie
Stylists: Joyce Mason and Tessa Paul

For this volume:
Designer: Barbara Borup
Writer: Lesley Dore
Editorial Assistants: Hannah Beardon and Paul Thompson

Printed in Italy

Adult supervision advised for all crafts and recipes,
particularly those involving sharp instruments and heat.

CONTENTS

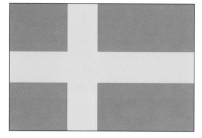

SWEDEN:

Sweden lies in the far north of Europe. It is a long, thin country, and its most northern areas reach as far as the Arctic Circle. Here the freezing cold winter days are dark for the whole of their 24 hours.

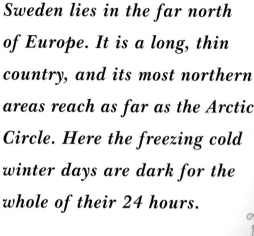

Mt. Kebne

Jokkmokk

Skellefteå

Norwegian Sea

Umeälven

Indalsälven

Sweden

Gulf of Bothnia

Norway

Uppsala

STOCKHOLM

Denmark

Baltic Sea

▲**Herds of reindeer** are reared by the people of Lappland. They move the animals with the seasons in search of food supplies. During winter these animals dig deep into the snow to find the lichen that is their cold-weather diet.

First Impressions

- **Population** 8,794,000
- **Largest city** Stockholm with a population of 1,669,840
- **Longest river** Indalsälven
- **Highest mountain** Mt. Kebne at 6,926 ft.
- **Exports** Machinery, chemicals, iron and steel, paper, wood, vehicles
- **Capital city** Stockholm
- **Political status** Constitutional monarchy
- **Climate** Short, warm summers and long winters
- **Art and culture** Three of Sweden's most famous artists are the film-maker Ingmar Bergman, the playwright August Strindberg, and the painter Carl Larsson.

nland

▶**The old church** at Gamal, in Uppsala, holds the remains of the three Swedish kings Aun, Egil, and Adils. It was built in medieval times to replace the last of Scandanavia's pre-Christian temples. In this temple the heathens worshiped such gods as Thor and Odin.

◀**The Swedish capital, Stockholm,** was first mentioned in writing in 1252. The old city is colorful, with red and ocher facades. The modern city sprawls over a lake and a river mouth that leads into the Baltic Sea. To the east of Stockholm is an archipelago of thousands of tiny islands. .

RELIGIONS

Almost 500 years ago the Swedish Christians decided to break with the pope, and Protestantism became the national religion. To this day the vast majority of Swedes are members of the Church of Sweden.

CHRISTIANITY spread more slowly in Sweden than in other countries in Europe. The first Christian missionaries arrived in the ninth century to convert the people, but the Swedes remained faithful to their old gods. Another two centuries passed before Sweden could be called a Christian country.

The first Swedish Christians belonged to the Catholic faith. At the head of the church was the pope, who lived in Rome, but every town and village had its own priest. He told the people how they should worship God. Important events in the life of Jesus were observed by ceremonies or holidays, or by special rules pertaining to food. On some days the people were forbidden to eat meat or eggs. Around these Christian festivals and rituals grew many traditions, some of which were left over from the pagan gods. They were to do with nature and the seasons.

In 1527 there was another change in the religious lives of Swedish people. In Germany a scholar named Martin Luther began to protest against the Catholic Church. He believed that people should have their own relationship with God and worship Him more simply. He did not accept the pope as head of the church. This movement became known as Protestantism.

Luther's followers believed in many of the same things as Catholics, but they gave up some of the rituals. Swedes thought Luther's ideas about worshipping God were correct and so they became Protestants. Today almost all Swedes are Lutheran Protestants, but in their festivals there are the remnants of Catholic practices.

GREETINGS FROM **SWEDEN!**

Sweden is one of Europe's largest countries, but very few people live there — the whole country's population is just a little more than that of New Jersey! Sweden is a highly industrialized country, and its factories produce steel, electrical machinery, aircraft, and vehicles. Most of the farmlands are in the south, and the farmers can almost provide enough food to feed all the people. The vast Swedish forests supply plenty of valuable timber for wood.

The Swedish language belongs to the Germanic languages and has similarities with German and English. The Finnish and Lapp minorities in the north of Sweden speak Finnish and Saami. Since Swedish is not spoken anywhere else in the world, it is important for Swedish children to learn foreign languages at school. Their first foreign language is English, and later on either German, French, or Spanish is added.

How do you say...

Hello

Hej

How are you?

Hur mår du?

My name is...

Jag heter...

Goodbye

Hejdå

Thank you

Tack

Peace

Fred

EASTER

Easter is the religious festival that marks the death and resurrection of Jesus Christ. Since it falls in the spring, the Swedes also celebrate the end of their long, dark winter.

The six weeks that lead up to Easter are called Lent. During this time the bakeries are full of Lenten Buns, bread rolls filled with marzipan paste and cream.

Lenten twigs are sold on the market stalls. These are birch twigs with brightly colored feathers tied to the ends. When the twigs are put into water, the yellowish-green leaves come out. They are reminders of the new life of spring, and also of the whipping of Jesus Christ before He was crucified.

Swedish families like to visit each other at Easter. In preparation the houses are filled with yellow and pink decorations. The curtains and tablecloths follow this color scheme. Daffodils and tulips are put in vases.

As in many other Christian countries, it is traditional to eat decorated hard-boiled eggs. An old way of coloring the shells is to use onion peel, ears of

LENTEN BUNS

MAKES EIGHT

6 soft round white bread rolls
Confectioners' sugar
2½ ounces marzipan or almond paste
½ cup whipping cream
Cinnamon

Cut a small section off tops of rolls and put them aside. With a teaspoon, dig a hollow in the base of each roll. On a work surface dusted with confectioners' sugar, knead marzipan until soft. Cut into six pieces and shape each piece to fit the hollow. Whip the cream until soft peaks form. Put a big spoonful of cream into each roll on top of marzipan. Replace tops of rolls. Dust with confectioners' sugar mixed with a little cinnamon.

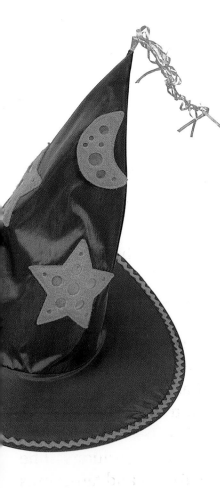

On Easter Saturday little girls all over Sweden have great fun dressing up as wicked Easter witches.

long bright skirts. They go around the streets and visit neighbors' houses. They carry a big coffeepot and beg for money, chocolates, and candies. They fill the pot with goodies.

This game relates to an ancient belief in witchcraft. The custom dates back to an old superstition that on the evening before Good Friday, the day Jesus was crucified, the witches flew off on their broomsticks to meet the Devil on the "Blue Mountain."

In some areas of the country people let off noisy firecrackers and light bonfires on Easter Eve to scare away the witches.

corn, or birch leaves. The plants and eggs are boiled together. The plant color makes patterns on the shells.

On Easter Eve little girls dress up as Easter witches. They paint their faces with large red spots and wear

Yellow feathers give the bare branches of birch some color before the buds begin to show. Yellow daffodils and pink tulips herald the arrival of Easter and the spring weather.

END-OF-SCHOOL YEAR

Graduation is treated with great respect and joy in Sweden. The whole country celebrates with those students who are finally leaving their school, and their childhood, behind them.

Celebrations and parties in the middle of June mark the end of the school year and the beginning of the long-awaited summer.

Every school has an end-of-year assembly where the pupils, wearing their very best clothes, sing traditional summer songs, such as "The Time of Flowers Is Coming." These children will not have to return to school until the second or third week in August.

The students who are finishing secondary school at the age of 18 or 19 have a more elaborate celebration. There is a prize-giving ceremony with performances of music and drama and good luck speeches from the teachers. The "fully fledged" high school graduates put on a white peaked cap to show they have graduated. They will wear it for the rest of the day.

When they leave the school building, all the parents are waiting for them at the school gate. The parents greet their sons and

Proud parents show childhood photographs of the graduates. These pictures may be the source of jokes or happy memories on this special day when the students officially become adults.

THE SMÖRGASBORD

No end-of-school party is complete without a smörgasbord. This is a type of festive buffet that means "sandwich table." Usually there are plates and plates of open-faced sandwiches made with smoked meats and fish, egg, and bits of garnishes. It is delicious, but not something that Swedes have every day.

daughters with flowers and champagne and hold up signs with a childhood photograph and their child's name.

The students like to drive in groups around the town, sitting in open-top cars decorated with flowers and greenery. There is a lot of excitement, noise, and laughter. In the evening the celebrations continue at parties and balls.

After graduation the white caps, called *studentmossor*, are worn every year on the evening of April 30, known as Walpurgis Night, when Swedes still follow the old tradition of lighting a bonfire and listening to choral singing.

In Uppsala, the oldest university town in Sweden, thousands of students march through the old town, wearing their white caps and singing songs about the coming of spring.

High school graduates wear these white caps at their graduation and later on at the Walpurgis Night celebrations.

MIDSOMMAR

Midsummer Day is the biggest summer festival in Sweden. It celebrates the solstice, the longest day of the year.

Midsommar, or Midsummer Day, falls on the weekend that is closest to June 24. The festival has no religious significance. It probably originated in pagan times when the summer solstice was celebrated.

Families and their friends travel out into the countryside to enjoy the long, warm days. In the north of Sweden the sun does not really set at all.

For children the holiday begins in the afternoon when the "midsummer pole" is raised. Everyone helps to dress the pole with wild flowers and lots of greenery.

The pole is the focal point of the party. Children hold hands and dance around it. They play traditional games in which they pretend to be little animals.

As the evening draws on, a meal of

The midsummer pole is similar to maypoles seen in Germany and other countries. The difference is in the proud display of the national flag. The horse is a traditional Swedish toy.

boiled new potatoes and herring is served, with strawberries and ice cream for dessert.

The music begins, and people dance until dawn. Young girls pick wild flowers that night and place them under their pillows. It is said they will then dream of the man they will marry.

Swedes wear their folk costumes and dance to folk music. The sound of the concertina is often heard at these festivities.

THE NATIONAL ANTHEM
Thou ancient, thou freeborn, thou mountainous North, In beauty and peace our hearts beguiling, I greet thee, thou loveliest land on Earth, Thy sun, thy skies, thy verdant meadows smiling (repeat)

DU GAMLA, DU FRIA

Du gam - la, du fri - a, du fjäll - hö - ga Nord, du

tys - ta, du gläd - je - ri - ka skö - na! Jag häl - sar dig, vä - nas - te

land__ u p - pa jord, din sol, din him - mel, di - na äng - der

gröp - na, din sol din him - mel, di - na äng - der grö - na.

THE JOKKMOKK FAIR

For nearly 400 years the Lapps have met for their annual market fair in Jokkmokk, a town on the edge of the Arctic Circle. Today many tourists travel north to attend the unique event.

Lappland is a region that covers north-ern Scandinavia. It is inhabited by the Lapps, or Saami people, who settled here in ancient times. Today about 17,000 Saami people live in Sweden.

To this day many Saami keep herds of reindeer. They seldom take a rest from the care of the reindeer. However, when the winter days are at their very coldest, the Saami pause for a few days and gather together.

Ever since 1605 the Lapps have met in Jokkmokk for a big fair. This gathering traditionally happens in February, before the reindeer herds trek to the mountains for spring and summer.

Stalls are set up selling reindeer skin boots and gloves, and knives with handles made from reindeer horn. There are finely decorated coffee cups and beautiful woven

clothes. Reindeer meat and other Lapp delicacies are prepared at the food stalls.

The highlight of the fair is the reindeer race. Everyone gathers on the shore of the frozen lake to watch. Sometimes the spectators have to scatter as the animals skid off course. People warm themselves with black coffee served with salt. They sing *joiks*, light-hearted songs that they make up on the spot.

Reindeer supply the food and clothing of many Lapps but the animals also bring sport. Reindeer races are great fun.

TRADITIONAL LIFE

Until fairly recently all Lapp reindeer breeders led a nomadic life, which means they moved around all year, searching for food for their animals. The whole family followed the herd up the mountains in spring. All the provisions, tents, and even huts were packed onto sleighs or the backs of the reindeer. Lapp families drank reindeer milk, ate reindeer meat, and wore clothes made from reindeer skin.

Winter is the hardest time for both the animals and the herdsmen. The Arctic sun never rises, and the ground is snow-covered and frozen. The animals dig deep into the snow crust to find lichen, the most important food in the reindeers' diet.

Today reindeer herding is still the Lapps' main livelihood, but only the men follow the herd, and helicopters and snowmobiles make their job a lot easier.

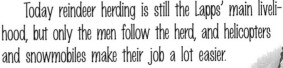

THE BEAR'S TAIL

Fishermen in Lappland have to drill holes in the frozen lakes to fish through the ice. A popular Swedish folk tale tells of how a bear lost his tail when he tried to fish in the same way.

ONE WINTER'S DAY Bear was getting hungry and was thinking about his dinner as he walked through the forest. Suddenly, he met Fox, running along with a string of fish hanging from his mouth. Fox obviously couldn't wait to get to a quiet place and devour the fish for his dinner. He had stolen them from a fisherman on the lake.

"Where did you get those fish?" asked Bear. He loved fish, but he rarely managed to catch any himself.

"I caught them, of course. What do you think?" answered Fox. "It's the easiest thing in the world. The lake is teeming with all kinds of fish."

"Please tell me how you did it, though," asked Bear. "I would like to have fish for my dinner. But whenever I try and catch a fish it slips out of my paws at the very last moment."

"You're doing it the wrong way," said Fox. "I'll tell you what to do. Go out on the ice and make a hole the way man does. When you've made the hole in the ice, drop in your tail and sit very, very quietly. The fish will come, one by one, and nibble your tail. It will tingle a bit, but don't worry. Just think of your supper."

"The longer you sit there, the more fish will come. When you are sure you have plenty, then pull sideways – very hard – with all your strength. Out will come your tail, and out will come all the fish to make a splendid feast."

So off Bear went to the lake. He did what Fox had told him to do. He made a hole in the ice and sat quietly waiting for the fish to take the bait. He was hungry and hoped for a lot of fish.

He sat there for such a long time that his tail became completely frozen. When he finally couldn't stand the cold any more and pulled sideways, very hard as he had been told, his beautiful long tail snapped off. And that is why, to this day, Bear has only a short, stumpy tail.

NATIONALDAG

Since 1916, June 6 has been celebrated as the Swedish Flag Day. However, this day became National Day in 1983.

For a long time Sweden did not have a national day as most other countries do. It wasn't until the beginning of this century that the Swedish people wanted to show openly the love and pride they felt for their country.

So in 1916 the first Swedish Flag Day was celebrated on June 6. The date was chosen for two reasons. Firstly, because Gustav Vasa was elected King of Sweden on that day in 1523. Secondly, because a new Swedish constitution was signed on June 6 in 1809.

Gustav Vasa was a young nobleman who led an uprising against the Danes, who had ruled Sweden for over 100 years. He was able to escape from his persecutors by skiing across 55 miles of hazardous countryside. Every year in March a skiing race is held to commemorate this feat, and today as many as 12,000 people take part in it.

From 1916 onward the formal celebration of National Flag Day in the capital took place at the Stockholm Stadium. Here the king would

Swedes treasure their folk costumes. The costumes are often heirlooms, and the designs differ between provinces. Even the queen of Sweden wears traditional dress on National Day.

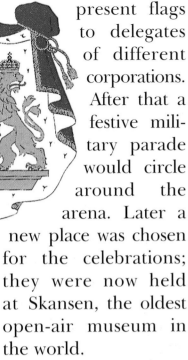

present flags to delegates of different corporations. After that a festive military parade would circle around the arena. Later a new place was chosen for the celebrations; they were now held at Skansen, the oldest open-air museum in the world.

In 1983 Flag Day was named *Nationaldag*, or "National Day." It is not a public holiday as in other countries. The celebrations in Sweden are usually held in the evening when most people have finished their working day.

In many places all over Sweden there are parades and speeches, and the flag is flown everywhere. However, the former military element has almost disappeared. All the royal family attend

the presentation of flags at Skansen.

Swedes love to fly their blue and yellow flags. Most houses have their own flag-pole. In towns people who live in apart-ments fly flags from their balconies.

The design of the Swedish flag is based on the Swedish Coat of Arms, which is blue divided quarterly by a cross of gold. The Greater Coat of Arms (left) is used by the king.

JANSSON'S TEMPTATION

SERVES 8
1 t. oil
7 medium potatoes, peeled
2 T. butter, cut into pieces
2 onions, diced
16 sardines, rinsed and dried
1½ cups milk

Preheat the oven to 375° F. Grease a 9" x 11" baking pan with oil. Cut the potatoes into very thin slices. You may need an adult to help you. Spread half the potatoes over the base of the pan. Sprinkle the diced onion over them. Then put the sardines on top. Cover with the remaining half of the potatoes. Sprinkle with pepper and dot with butter. Pour the milk over the top. Bake until the potatoes are soft and the milk has been absorbed, about 60 minutes.

WEAVE A PAPER BASKET

People living on farms or in remote villages used to make their own baskets from grasses. This basket is made from cardboard and is strong enough to hold a little store of candy.

Most people enjoy the convenience of factory-made things, but until recently many people made their own cloth and wove their own baskets. In the remote mountain settlements of Sweden some people still weave baskets. They use grass and reeds, but they make them the same way as we describe for this cardboard basket.

YOU WILL NEED
Thin cardboard
Scissors
Staple gun
Ruler

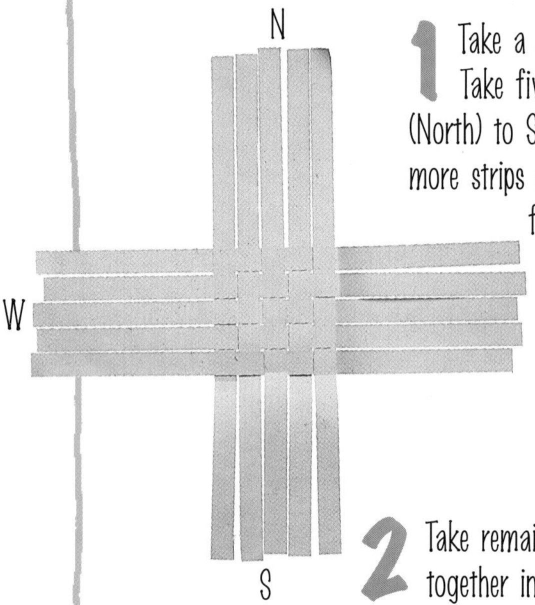

1 Take a sheet of thin cardboard and cut 16 strips 1" x 16." Take five of the strips and place them side by side N (North) to S (South) as shown in diagram to the left. Take five more strips and weave them W (West) to E (East) through the first five to make the base of the basket.

2 Take remaining six strips and glue them together in pairs to make 3 long strips. Weave these strips into the unwoven lengths of N and S. Bend the longer strips round corners. The lengths of N and S are forced into a vertical position. This weaving forms the sides of the basket.

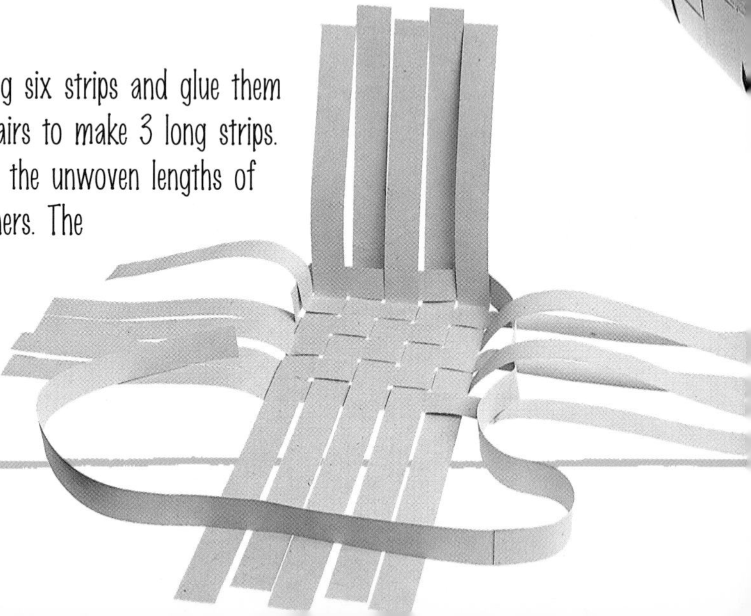

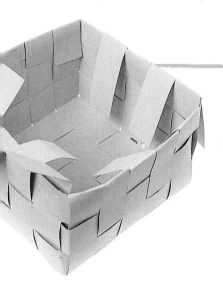

3 Weave these strips so that the sides of the basket are three strips deep. Fold the unwoven lengths of these strips into the interior of the basket. Weave them into the sides.

4 Cut three strips of thin card 14" x 2". Fold them in half lengthways and position two of them over the top edge of the basket, folding them at the corners. This forms a secure binding to the basket edges.

5 Take the third strip and curve it to make a handle. Position it in place. Use a staple gun to secure both the handle and the binding edge. You now have a pretty woven basket to hold candy, cookies, or jewelry.

6 Fill the basket with flowers or cakes. You could give it to someone as an attractive gift.

LUCIADAG

*Lucia Day falls on December 13.
Although named after a Sicilian saint,
this festival is not a religious event.*

The festival known as *Luciadag*, or "Lucia Day," with its pretty procession, is a much-loved tradition in Sweden, but its origins are hard to trace. The festival has nothing to do with the saint Lucia. It is unique to Sweden, and is not celebrated in any other country.

In every town and village a young girl, usually with long blonde hair, is chosen to represent Lucia. The girl is dressed in a full-length white gown with a red sash tied around the waist. Her crown has candles and lingonberry twigs. When the candles are lit, they create a halo effect.

Lucia leads a line of girls

The Lucia procession winding through the dark, snowy streets is a beautiful sight.

and boys down the street. They also wear white robes and carry candles. Some of the boys, called "star boys," wear pointed hats decorated with gold stars. As they walk, they sing the "Sankta Lucia," a much-loved folk song. This title means "Saint Lucia."

Lucia and her attendants visit homes for the elderly, schools, and hospitals. They take gingersnaps and saffron-flavored buns to give as presents. These are known as "Lucia cats."

Many families will start the day very early with a breakfast of Lucia cats and coffee.

Mothers or brothers and sisters dress the youngest girl as Lucia. She then sings the Lucia song and carries the tray of special buns.

The Lucia festival may have come from Germany. In the seventeenth and eighteenth centuries a girl dressed as the Christ Child in a white tunic with a wreath of candles in her hair used to give out presents.

The night falls heavily around the farm and the barns.
Around the earth the sun forgot, the shadows linger.
Then in our house arises, with lighted candles, Saint Lucia, Saint Lucia.

SANKTA LUCIA

Nat - ten gar tung -a fjät runt gard och stu - va.

Kring jord, som sol'n för - lät, skug - - gor - na

ru - va. Da i vart mör - ka hus sti - ger med

tän - da ljus Sanc - ta —— Lu - ci - a,

1. Sanc - ta Lu - ci - a, 2. Sanc - ta Lu - ci - a.

SANKTA LUCIA

Lucia *is the Latin word for "light." Blind people pray to her to rescue them from the dark world of their affliction.*

LONG AGO IN Roman times Lucia sat in her courtyard watching the water in the fountain. That morning the goldsmith had called, and she had chosen the beautiful coronet that would adorn her hair on her wedding day. But Lucia was not dreaming of her lover. She had expereinced a miracle, and she felt that this would change her life more than her forthcoming marriage.

Her confusion started with her mother's illness. All the best doctors in Syracuse in Italy had failed to cure her. "Before I die," she said, "I will visit the tomb of St. Agatha. She, like me, was a Christian. She will help me to feel at peace with the world."

So Lucia and her mother traveled south along the road to Catamia. They were very careful to keep the purpose of their visit secret, as the practising of Christianity was strictly forbidden. Diocletian, who ruled the Roman Empire at that time, tried to stamp out the Christian faith by killing those who believed in Christ. He wanted everyone to worship only the Roman gods and to worship him as a god on Earth.

When they reached St. Agatha's tomb, the two women knelt down. As they prayed to the saint, Lucia's sick mother was miraculously cured. She returned home healthy and happy.

Lucia wanted to show her deep gratitude to God for making her mother well. Jesus had lived a simple life, sharing what little he had with others. Lucia was rich. She decided to part with all her wealth. Taking all her beautiful clothes, her jewels, and her

money, she went out into the streets of Syracuse and gave them all away.

When her fiancé heard of her actions, he was furious with her. "What have you done?" he cried. "We were rich. How can I marry a penniless bride?"

Lucia smiled. "Jesus was poor. I don't want a life of luxury. I want to follow His ways. I will not marry you!"

"I'll tell the judge you're a Christian!" raged her fiancé.

The judge told Lucia to give up Jesus, but Lucia refused. The judge then ordered that Lucia be tied to a team of oxen and then be dragged away from her home. Lucia stood firm, her eyes closed in prayer. Although the strong animals pulled with all their might, they could not move the young girl. In the end the judge's men thrust a dagger through her throat. Lucia was a martyr who died for her faith.

CHRISTMAS

Swedes like to make Christmas last a long time. It begins with the season of Advent and lasts until January 13, when the decorations are taken down.

At the end of November the family gets out the Advent candlestick. These used to be lit up with candles. Nowadays electric bulbs are used.

Preparations for Christmas really begin after Saint Lucia Day. Trees sold on street corners are brought home to be decorated with figures of Father Christmas, stars, and angels. Little goats made from straw or biscuit dough are traditional Swedish Christmas decorations. Sprigs of greenery are twisted into garlands for the front door. Little boxes of logs and candles stand behind angel figures.

One of the special treats for the younger children is the gingerbread house. Its roof tiles, its doors, and its windows are outlined in white frosting.

Families visit their relatives. The festivities begin on December 24 with a lunch of broth and bread.

In the evening the traditional Christmas dinner begins with a smörgasbord of liver paste, pickled herring, and smoked sausage. This is followed by hot foods such as meatballs and ham. Christmas dessert is a rice porridge with an almond hidden inside. The person who finds the almond must say a "porridge rhyme."

Father Christmas is really a newcomer in Sweden. Traditionally, the *jultomten*, the Swedish Christmas gnome, delivers a sack of festive presents. One of the men in the family dresses up as the jultomten. He knocks on the door and asks if the children have been good, then he hands out gifts.

On Christmas Day candlelit church services start at 7 o'clock in the morning. Afterwards, people spend the day at home. One tradition children love is when the whole family joins hands to dance around the tree and then, in a long line, everybody dances through all the rooms in the house.

Their tree is left up until January 13. The children then strip the tree and throw it into the street. This is the sign that Christmas is finally over.

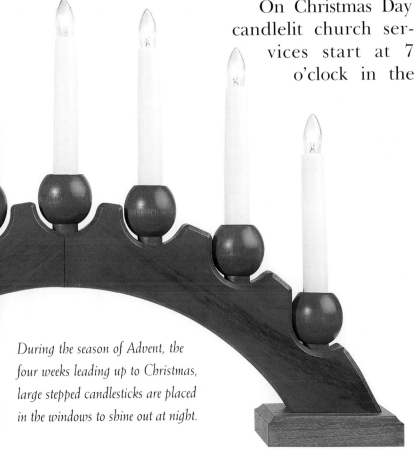

During the season of Advent, the four weeks leading up to Christmas, large stepped candlesticks are placed in the windows to shine out at night.

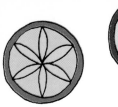

MAKE A YULE BOX

Christmas decorations include a little yule box, placed on windows, mantels, or tables. Often the box is surrounded by plaster angels dressed in blue.

Christmas falls in the dead of winter in Sweden. For centuries buildings were kept warm by great logs of fire. Nowadays most places have central heating. However, the memories of the old Christmas fires are kept alive with models of fir branches and cones. Make a yule box as a winter gift symbolizing warmth.

1 Cut three pieces of stiff cardboard 16" x 3". These form the long sides and base of the box. Cut two pieces 3" x 3". These form the short ends. Glue and tape the five sections of the box together.

2 Tear strips of newspaper. Glue and layer them all over the box. Make about 3 layers. Let glue dry.

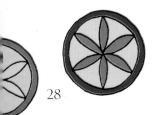

3 Paint the box white. This will give the paper-covered box a smooth surface and a good base on which to paint your design. Trace your design or draw it straight onto the box. Color your design with paints. Fill in large areas of color first. Wait for the paint to dry then apply a thin varnish with all-purpose glue.

4 Cut the oasis to fit the box and place it firmly in box. Push four candles into the oasis. Arrange the fir cones, fir needles, and spruce around the candles. Place your yule box in a window or on a mantel or table as an attractive Christmas decoration.

29

KRÄFTOR

*Crayfish parties are held in August. They are called **Kräftor**. People sit outside in the moonlight and celebrate the beginning of the crayfish season with a special feast.*

In August, when the holidays are drawing to a close, people get together with their friends to enjoy eating crayfish.

Crayfish from the lakes of central Sweden are said to have the best flavor of any in the world. A hundred years ago so many were caught that the government limited the fishing season to a couple of months in the autumn.

The night of the full moon is the best night for the crayfish party, as people like to sit outside. Paper lanterns with moon faces are suspended over the table. The boiled crayfish are piled onto dishes and served with different sauces. The parties are very happy and informal, and people eat, sing, and recite poems late into the night.

WORDS TO KNOW

Advent: The period beginning four Sundays before Christmas.

Coronet: A small crown or a headdress.

Crayfish: A small lobsterlike shellfish.

Graduation: A ceremony in which certificates are awarded to students who have completed a course of study.

Industrialized: A country with many factories producing manmade goods.

Lapps: The Saami people of Lappland in northern Scandinavia.

Lent: The 40 days between Ash Wednesday and Easter.

Martyr: A person who is put to death for refusing to give up his or her faith.

Missionary: A person who travels with the aim of converting others to his or her religion.

Nomads: People who travel all or some of the time in search of food for their animals.

Pagan: A name given to the religions followed in Europe before the arrival of Christianity.

Protestant: A member of one of the Protestant churches, which together form one of the main branches of Christianity. The Protestants split from the Roman Catholic Church in the sixteenth century.

Resurrection: The rising of Christ from the dead on Easter Sunday.

Roman Catholic: A member of the Roman Catholic Church, the largest branch of Christianity. The head of this church is the pope.

Smörgasbord: Delicate open sandwiches served before a meal or as a buffet.

Summer solstice: The longest day of the year.

Winter solstice: The shortest day of the year.

ACKNOWLEDGMENTS

WITH THANKS TO:
Lesley Dore. Kilburn Accordions, London. Midsummer pole and folk doll by Zoë Paul.

PHOTOGRAPHY:
All photographs by Bruce Mackie except: Marshall Cavendish pp. 12, 19. Cover photograph by Korky.

ILLUSTRATIONS BY:
Fiona Saunders pp. 4 – 5. Tracy Rich p. 7. Maps by John Woolford.

Recipes: Ellen Dupont.

SET CONTENTS